THE ARCH

THE ARCH

▲

PHOTOGRAPHS BY JOEL MEYEROWITZ

**ESSAYS BY JOEL MEYEROWITZ
AND VIVIAN BOWER**

A NEW YORK GRAPHIC SOCIETY BOOK

LITTLE, BROWN AND COMPANY • BOSTON

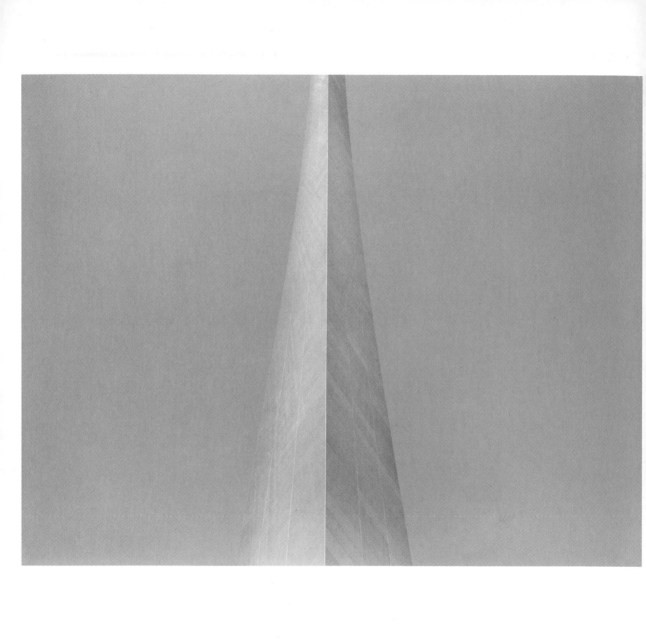

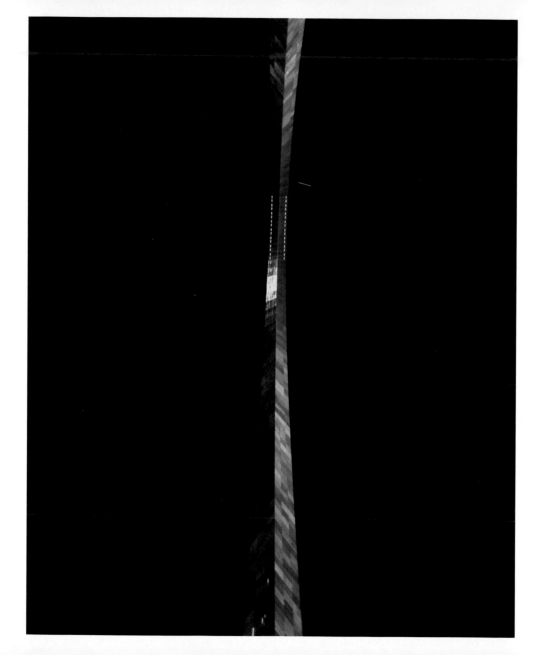

SAINT LOUIS & THE ARCH

▲

JOEL MEYEROWITZ

The storm came out of the north and brought its darkening skies to meet those of nightfall from the east. In between, in a shred of fading blue, the moon was rising, showing yellow over the waxy pink haze on the horizon. The wind carried the smell of the plains, dampened slightly as it puffed its way down the river's valley. A few stray people, lingering downtown after work, ran for their cars. One man, across the street, saw me embracing my camera and tripod against the wind. He pointed to the sky and yelled something to caution me, but his words were carried away by the wind. I hadn't come to St. Louis to be cautious. I left the shelter of the buildings and walked down to the large space around the Arch, near the river, to see the storm. It was my first day in St. Louis. I knew I was in the right place.

I like cities: there is a wildness to them, a sense of the unknown, something like nature. I came to St. Louis to photograph, with no preconceptions or desire to pass judgment. I had the advantage of being a stranger in the city. For me all things were equal. I had the pleasure then of discovering the streets and naming the parts. Only with time do the things that have meaning become apparent. The themes and inventions that emerge reflect the response and vulnerability of the observer. I trusted my instinct to guide me to where feeling was strongest. There I stopped and looked hard. Photography has taught me to pay close attention, which is what I demand when looking at photographs. I am most pleased when a photograph allows one to enter in, in an evenhanded way, where time can be spent, just looking.

On any given day in St. Louis I was excited, surprised, lonely, fatigued, entranced, saddened, or moved. I was stimulated by the city. I pushed hard and the city offered the best resistance, the kind you hope to find in a dancing partner. As we whirled I saw many sides, as if other cities exist here, all with the same name, each different, depending on the approach I took and how I felt on any given day.

Apart from the city is the Arch. I found it deeply moving, profound. There were days when, standing beneath it, I felt I knew the power of the pyramids. It was restorative, contemplative. It was more than a technological marvel or a symbol. It was pure form, the beauty of mathematics, a drawing on the heavens, perfect pitch. I came to be in awe of it. Once, while passing through its center, I stood at the place where sound would emerge if it were a tuning fork. I felt the vibration in the air. Once, I cried, for no reason. With all of its sameness, I could stalk around it and it was never the same. It was a sundial. Light and color made their way over its surface. I have seen the Arch change from a white you could not look at to black, in broad daylight. I've seen it disappear, reflect like a mirror, and turn pink, sometimes all in one day. I remembered mountains doing that.

I watched what people did when they came to see the Arch and was surprised by the forms their ritual behavior took. Most visitors press their bodies against it, give themselves over to it. With their arms up in a flying position, they appear ready to glide over its surface. At the least they press a cheek or trail a hand across its flank. Some people divide themselves along its knife edge, fearless, but still thrilled by its hardness. The thing is invulnerable. One cannot get a hand hold on it. Its smallest part is bigger than any of us. Standing beside it, one sees human scale diminish as when a figure stands at the ocean's edge. It contains the space that cathedrals aspire to. You feel it most when you submit to it.

Below the Arch, down at the Mississippi's edge, one can look back and there is no city visible. Standing within the city, one does not know that the river exists. St. Louis has moved back from the river. Its life no longer depends on it. The Arch now is the source of its symbolic pride. I walked along the river every day. It did not have the power over me that the Arch had, except once, when I stood amid the driftwood. Whole trees were thrown on the cobbled bank, with cars parked precariously among them. Instantly, I saw where I was: a boneyard at the foot of the Arch! Around me were the leavings of forests far to the north. The river was distinctly different from the Arch, less spiritual, more real.

St. Louis never disappointed me. She was there at every turn. Turn from the river with your back to the east, and you can see the dust of the prairies granulating the light. I'm tempted to say ululating, for there is a persistent tremor in the light at that particular point in our geography where St. Louis rests. There is no other place like it.

A BRIEF HISTORY

▲

VIVIAN BOWER

The Gateway Arch is a magnificent symbol of Saint Louis's role as the gateway to the west. It stands on the site where, in 1764, French explorer Pierre Laclede established a trading post. That settlement became a departure point for explorers, pioneers, fur traders and others who were part of the country's westward movement. After the signing of the Louisiana Purchase in 1803, which annexed to the Union a large portion of the middle United States, it was clear that Saint Louis, in its strategically located setting, would continue to play a major role in western expansion.

In the 1930's, Saint Louis civic leaders had a vision to transform Laclede's landing, a now decaying section of the City, into a 91 acre park with a memorial honoring Thomas Jefferson, the Louisiana Purchase, and the city itself. A nationwide architectural competition was sponsored by the Jefferson National Expansion Memorial.

Most entrants produced conventional designs of the time, such as a pylon or a slab and a statue. It was Eero Saarinen, a Finnish-American architect, whose design was awarded first prize. Only Saarinen's visionary design, a stainless steel arch leaping out of a forest along the banks of the Mississippi, carried the message of the future, both in form and material. While appreciating the extraordinary presence of the arch, it is important to remember the city planners whose desire found its expression in Saarinen's vision.

Saarinen said, "The major concern here was to create a monument which would have lasting significance and would be a landmark of our time. An absolutely simple shape—such as the Egyptian pyramids or obelisks—seemed to be the basis of the great memorials that have kept their significance and dignity across time." His design was an inverted three-sided catenary curve, a shape arrived at by hanging a chain freely between two supporting points and projecting this curve upward to form an arch. The weight and thrust of the arch passes through the lower portion of the legs and is absorbed into the foundation, making it strong enough to sway no more than 18 inches in a 150 mile per hour wind. Saarinen believed this pure form continued in the tradition of all great monuments that have been basic geometric shapes. He also felt that "the mathematical precision seemed to enhance the timelessness of the form, but at the same time its dynamic quality seemed to link it to our own time."

Unfortunately, Saarinen didn't live to see the arch completed. It was to take thirty years to secure government funds, to clear the land and relocate the elevated railroad, before construction could actually begin.

The arch was to span a height of 630 feet. Each of the legs was designed as an equilateral triangle, 54 feet on a side at the base by 12 feet high, tapering to a triangle of 17 feet by 8 feet at the top. All together there were to be 71 sections in each leg. (These sections were fabricated in Pennsylvania and shipped by rail to Saint Louis.) Inside of each section were double steel walls. At ground level the walls were 3 feet apart, but by the time the arch was at the 400 foot level, they were less than an inch apart. This construction left a core 48 feet wide at the base, narrowing to 15½ feet at the top. To reinforce the lower half, steel rods embedded in concrete were used. Above the 300 foot level, the concrete was discontinued and steel stiffeners were inserted.

On June 17, 1962, the work on the foundation began. Concrete was poured to a depth of 60 feet below ground level, the lower 30 feet being embedded in the bedrock. Nearly 26,000 tons of concrete were used on the foundation alone. By February 12, 1963, builders were ready to place the first stainless steel sections of the arch in the south leg. The first six sections of each leg were put in place by a crane, but because of its curve, further work on the arch posed challenging engineering problems. Once the sections had been placed as far as the ground cranes could reach, how would construction proceed?

Considering that the arch legs were 630 feet apart at the base and the uprights were expected to meet 630 feet in the air, new construction techniques had to be conceived. The MacDonald Construction Co. of Saint Louis, working with the Pittsburgh-DesMoines Steel Co., arrived at this solution—a creeper crane, which until then had only been used a few times. This creeper crane—an 80 ton tilted platform mounted on tracks that were attached to the arch—supported a 130 foot derrick. The crane would actually crawl up the sides of the arch, allowing new arch sections to be put in place and providing a platform from which to mount new tracks so that the crane could continue its ascent.

Given the deviation expected during construction, unavoidable because of expansion brought on by temperature changes and possible construction error, another device had to be developed that would give support to the uprights beyond the 530 foot level. To solve this problem, a stabilizing strut—like a bridge—was inserted between the two sections to support the legs and prevent swaying. At the final moment, another device, a spreader jack, was placed in the last 2 foot gap between the legs, stretching the legs, (which because of their weight—8,000 tons each—were leaning inward). This allowed the keystone, the final and top section, to be inserted. One of the most exciting moments in the construction of the arch was the placement of the keystone, which occurred on October 28, 1965. To avoid complications from the expansion of the steel by the sun's heat, placement began about 9:30 a.m. that day. The fire department was called in to spray cold water down the side of the south leg to try to prevent any additional expansion from direct exposure to the sun. It took only 13 minutes to raise the final 8 foot section to the top of the arch. By noon, the keystone was in place. It had taken only a little more than three years to accomplish the monumental task of constructing the Gateway Arch. Once the keystone was in place and welded, the jacks and tracking were removed and the surface was polished. The entire arch, including steel and concrete, weighed 16,678 tons. On October 29, 1965, the arch was completed.

Simple in design, the arch is an elegant and powerful image rising above the city. It's surface, opaque and reflective, follows the path of the sun, describes the mood of the day, and by nightfall comes alive with the reflection of the city's lights. Saarinen said, "The arch could be a triumphal arch for our age as the triumphal arches of classical antiquity were for theirs. Lofty, dynamic, of permanent significance, the arch could be a proper visual center and focus for the park, and as "The Gateway to the West," it could symbolize the spirit of the whole Memorial."

Published in association with Vivian Bower

First edition

A number of photographs reproduced in *The Arch* were originally published in *St. Louis & The Arch* (New York Graphic Society, 1980).

ISBN 0-8212-1724-0
Library of Congress Catalog Card Number 88-60985

New York Graphic Society books are published by
Little, Brown and Company (Inc.)
Published simultaneously in Canada by
Little, Brown & Company (Canada) Limited.

Designed by Jody Hanson, La Riviere · Hanson
Printed and bound by Acme Printing

PRINTED IN THE U.S.A.